Sky Thick With Fireflies
ETHNA McKIERNAN

salmonpoetry

Published in 2011 by
Salmon Poetry
Cliffs of Moher, County Clare, Ireland
Website: www.salmonpoetry.com
Email: info@salmonpoetry.com

ISBN 978-1-907056-88-8

COVER IMAGE: *Fireflies at night* © *Fernando Gregory | Dreamstime.com*
COVER DESIGN: *Siobhán Hutson*

Salmon Poetry receives financial support from
The Arts Council / An Chomhairle Ealaíon

for Pat, Pam and Jeff
and for my father

i.m.

*"If I do not remember thee, let my tongue
cleave to the roof of my mouth."*

PSALMS, CXXXVII, v. 6

Acknowledgements

The author is grateful for a 2011 Minnesota State Arts Board grant which allowed completion of this book. Ethna McKiernan is a fiscal year 2011 recipient of an Artist Initiative grant from the Minnesota State Arts Board. This activity is made possible in part by a grant from the Minnesota State Arts Board, through an appropriation by the Minnesota State Legislature and by a grant from the National Endowment for the Arts.

Some of these poems in this book have appeared in *Journal of Nature in Literature and Story*, *The Minnesota Poetry Calendar*, *New Hibernia Review*, *The Northstone Review*, *The Recorder*, *Salmon: A Journal in Poetry 1981-2007*, and the *St. Paul Almanac*. "Here" won the Donn Goodwin Prize in Poetry.

Thanks, as always, to my Warren Wilson MFA community.

Contents

SKY OF THE OTHERWORLD

SKY WITHOUT END

Here

"Somewhere you are writing or have written in
a room you came to as I come to this
room with honeyed corners…"

EAVAN BOLAND from
"The Rooms of Other Women Writers"

This is the place, Eavan, the kitchen
late at night, its untidy counters
heaped with books,

the boys asleep upstairs.
Here is where the first halting drafts appear
as the oven warms my feet

and here the blue midnight surges
through the window as it blends with stove-light
falling now upon the pages of Akhmatova.

Here lies the teenager's jacket dropped to the floor,
here the hardened spills of last night's meal.
Here's the stove-top which doubles

as my desk, and this is the room where
the light whir of wings can be heard
sometimes, an indiscriminate brush of air

blessing all that's ordinary – the spit of steam
rising from the kettle, my own bent shoulders
curved above the notebook. This is the room

in which my mother's ghost sings
as she kneads her soda bread, and right here
is the mortar of poetry, the plain materials of love.

SKY THAT GOT AWAY

The Sorrow-Flower

I am shopping in the supermarket
and an infant whimpers in the cereal aisle.
For a minute I recall the jolt of milk
trickling from my breasts eleven years ago,
that June of absences. I had refused
the medicine to dry the milk up, and my breasts
became great, swollen rocks of pain,
tender even to the touch of softest cotton
blouse. But I was stubborn and wild
for sensation; the rest of me, mind and heart,
anesthetized, numb. *After great pain,*
a formal feeling comes to shut the senses down,
and that burning in my nipples was the only thing
that made me know I was alive.
I look at the infant again but there is no let-down,
only the long regret I carry more lightly
these days than those, the sorrow-flower
I had sewn beneath my breasts
loosening its scarred hold on my chest.

Amniocentesis

That pulsing screen –
an ultrasound to find the spot
they could extract the illuminating fluid—

I remember Richard as remote,
afraid when he saw the needle
pierce my stomach
that my pain might be infectious.
I remember my own fear: was I too old
at 40, was the baby healthy,
was I wrong to think
love was the one boat
we could row through deep waters
and not drown?

The table was cold, the gel on my belly
was cold, the month-long wait for news
was winter tapping at my shoulder daily.
When they phoned to say *no
genetic problems, do you want
to go ahead?* I was skittery
with joy, blurting yes to the next
question, "*do you want to know
the child's gender?*"

A boy. Would a boy provide the glue
that kept a man who reasoned first
for abortion, fastened to us all?

Oh, hindsight is a sage –
I should have spent that pregnancy
studying the raccoon family
who slinked up from the river
to thieve garbage-treasure nightly

in the neighborhood that summer;
learning something from the way
the father ran when I shined
the flashlight in his panicked eyes,
two young cubs mewling
in the dust behind.

Birthmother to Her Sleeve

I've lost you since the day that you began.
Small spark begun as love, you changed
to inconvenience as you grew, your kinsman
father running toward the exit as arranged.

Small spark begun as love, you changed
from infant into boy. Great joy
you brought another family as arranged,
black grief I knew like Troy.

From infant into boy you caused great joy
for someone else. Not me. I missed you always
in the black grief I knew like Troy;
ruined, I unlearned the verb *to pray*.

For someone else, not me, you bloomed always,
no inconvenience as you grew, your kinsman
father ignorant of the verb to pray.
I've lost you since the day that you began.

Another of Her Unsent Letters

"Remorse—is memory—awake—
Her parties all astir."

EMILY DICKINSON, #744

The imprint of his infant head
upon her shoulder like a burn
that still scalds a decade later.

The downed plane flaming
only fields away from violet gentians
blooming from grey rock.

The salty coating in her throat
when, two days old,
she handed him away.

That weight, her arm lifted.
Waving.
Goodbye.

And nothing, nothing,
reconciled.

Ritual

While the sky is still
slurry with stars, I labor
to dress him without waking him,
the soft hiss of zipper
burring open the pajama-suit,
his feet sliding free from the flannel
sockets, the small face awash
with sleep. Always I carry him
to the car to return him to them,
releasing him so many times
as I drive that by the first stoplight,
I know the moves cold. Each night
he goes back in that other set of clothes;
each night they are innocent of the theft.

These Days

Someone else inhabits my body,
mows the lawn, prepares bare dinners

for the boys. I watch her move
as if she knew what she were doing,

all the rote energy of survival
fierce at its work.

That effort – how it costs.

July 4th, Late

Late now, and rain flays the lake
like stones drilling holes in black glass.
His absence like a phantom limb, I break.

My older children sleep. For whose sake
do they keep one foot in childhood, what task?
Late now, rain flays the lake.

Across the water, fireworks. They take
me straight to terror, things vanishing, the past
an absence like a phantom limb. I break.

Can any child simply be mistake?
I take out my grief and polish its sorry brass.
Late now, rain flays the lake.

Like stars, the lights dazzle and leave, opaque
as morning fog rising now from grass.
His absence like a phantom limb, I break.

Can sun take the morning, remake
its torn edges into something seamless?
Late now, rain flays the lake.
His absence like a phantom limb, I break.

Rumpelstilskin's Version

More than anything I craved a child
of my own to raise
who would fill the empty cup I was
to my parents' thirst.
I stuttered and my lame leg dragged
beneath my britches. When
they looked at me, I knew ugliness
like a second skin.

That no woman would lie with me
is a fact not lightly borne,
so when I heard the miller's daughter
sobbing at the spindle late that night,
I thought that if I spun her straw to gold
she might feel something more
than just beholden to my kindness
and in time even come to love me.
I would weave her gold blankets
to use against the evening chill,
and we would hold the small thimble
of our happiness in bed each night,
blessing its abundance.

But still she shuddered when she looked
at me instead of smiled; still
I kept extracting promises from her
I knew she couldn't keep.

One day I finally gave it up
and went back to the forest, the idea
of our child vanishing like mica-flakes
to wind, the heavy bag of my hurt
weighting my shoulders down.

The morning that the bells pealed
the news of the king's son, I froze.
They said he was perfect, long, straight legs
and a pure cry fluid as a bird's. I know
it wasn't right but a debt was owed,
and I had to claim him as my prize.

These days when I overhear his mother call
for him in the forest where we hide,
I hear a sorrow in her voice deeper than my own.
But the boy has grown to love me
as I am, and by sunrise, the only trace of us

they'll find will be a random blaze of gold, straw
in a blue-jay's nest when the sun catches it,
hours after the boy and I have journeyed on.

Falling

All day I'd been skidding
toward the thin rim of despair, teetering
like the circus acrobat
who goes on anyway, the net gone.
There are moments to jump, I know that;
reasons to enter the fire and walk out cleansed,
just as times it's necessary
to seize the air like rope and not let go.

I felt raw — the wind bit at my skin,
every birdsong was wrong, my throat
harbored sand and fishbones,
purple lupines hurt me with their deep indifference
and their beauty, someone's death pressed
against my left shoulder, and I knew that
sorrow was feeding her horses again,
preparing the journey down.

I remembered the Jonestown dreams
I couldn't lose for months and the burn
on Conor's hand as he reached
for balance but grabbed instead the barbecue stand.
I remembered the flat tone war in Belfast took in time
as each day's gestures emptied to the next.
And I thought of the indigo of Devin's eyes
when he was born, how when he left my arms
two days later for another mother
that blue was the one raft I clung to.

Tell me how to unlearn fear —
how to tame the horse's bared eyes
and teeth until they're friends to me,
safe as my lover's hands. Tell me how to ride that horse
like my twin; how to plunge my feet
into his sides while we braid our own coarse hair
together to become one animal
at peace with falling.

April

for Kate Stanley

On the rural roadside,
the grey brush of trees
leaning toward green;

the sound a crocus
makes when surging
through black earth;

the scar on the heart
no longer pink
but silver now;

all the old renewals,
their ferocious tenderness,
their raw nudges –

imperative, their yes.

SKY BELONGING TO US ALL

The Peacock Has a Hundred Eyes

Blue ovoids framed by yellow aureoles
signal to the female his readiness
to mate when his tail is raised.
Does the heavy train of feathers
prevent him from that lift, that radiant preen?
And what must the peahen think
walking through the clearing
into such a dazzling display, so many eyes
seducing her at once, so many tails
vying for the highest inch upward,
the widest arc of eyes outward?
Look, here comes one now, shaking himself
as if from a nap, wheeling his rainbow tail,
his bright salute of color, and all his hundred eyes
are looking at the shy peahen behind a bush
who has cast her dun-colored feathers down,
gaze averted from this surfeit of magnificence.

Narcissus at the Pond

I bent down,
my face so close
it grazed the surface
of the water.
My kingdoms hovered
above, below,
and a slight breeze
blew ripples of light
that quaked as the wind
rowed them toward me.

How I loved
what I saw!
Cloud-journeys,
a hummingbird's
red whir, the long arms
of the tree limb,
its black fingers
darkening the stones
below the water's seam,
the whole world
given twice.

The same moment
that I saw the world
that lived on water
I knew also
what lay below:
the fluid slipperiness
and teeth of fish,
the softness
of moss-covered wood
and pebble, every
aching hue my own.

And when
I raised my head
a few inches
he appeared,

his face swaying
and breaking apart
from its own beauty,
luminous. I touched
his cheek with my thumb
and he felt the weight
of my love for him,
his face shifting
to a dozen gorgeous faces
all at once.
Like an animal in fright,
completely still,
I held my breath
until he reappeared.

Sick with longing,
I think of him tonight,
like all nights, like all
days. To apprehend
such beauty and never
have it apprehend me –
to watch what I love
disintegrate from my touch –

I went back to the pond
in the winter and though
I rubbed the blurred ice
until a lighter circle formed,
I could not make him reappear.

Now the lilac's heady smell
has called me back again,
the ice gone, the water clear and sweet.
He was there. I didn't dare move
except to whisper of my passion...
Oh, my gazelle, my one
sky, my only glass
of ruby wine, how I love you!

His mouth
echoed the same words,
his lips moved exactly
as my own lips
moved, almost like a mirror.

And when I looked down
the last time,
he was crying, too.

Mrs. Magi Speaks

I scrub the children's linens and my own
against the grey rock by the shallow river,
wondering where I should begin.
With my husband's luminous robes,
bright and heady as the weight of gold
he plans to carry somewhere east of here in search of —
what? There's always trouble in the search;
some reckless folly named *star* calls him
and he sets out again. This time for a Jew,
a baby he believes will be the ruler, king
who'll shepherd my people Israel. O Gentile
husband John, do you belong among the planets
that you gaze on; what knowledge do you seek?
Here, I fret alone, nursing two children
through the night, tending olive trees and dried vegetables
by day in the desert sun, filling white pages
with these black scrawls when I can.
Today I wish you safety on the journey, love;
biting back my other wish that the heavens
and this stange new infant
felt not like another woman to me.
I scour the dust from the last of the garments,
damning gold, myrrh and frankincense
with each whipstroke of my arm.

Scissors

I always know where they're put away
in the kitchen drawer, though
I've left them sometimes on the floor
for days, abandoned next to tape and glue,
stars and paper, someone's project for school.
I love their light rasp when opened,
the tune they make when clicking shut.
What lives they've lived inside my hands,
those angled bows of orange plastic,
their gun-metal legs pointed below.
What witness they've borne to my journey,
the first to feel my braids falling
from my shoulders when I cut them
cleanly as my childhood at thirteen.
Such comfort that their snug fit provides
when slicing into new fabric
for a new dress, a new life; how helpful,
tonight, their blades, as I shred to bits
old letters, photographs,
every trace of the unwanted past.

Third Elegy

I miss you, Stephen, even now, decades
past the day you let the gun release
its last retort into your head.
Imagining your blond hair white
today, the flesh beneath your neck slack
and jowly, your imagination slowed
from manic to considered like a meteor
on lithium, I would still prefer
the fire absent from your eyes than
your absence. Old companion,
how the world diminished afterward
in places where you walked and shook
the seventies to dizzy bits
along the Mississippi water-flats
and streets of Minneapolis!
Tonight, this new and shaky century,
shakier somehow without you:
a bell is tolling *wrong, wrong, wrong.*

Jeff's Poem

For the Fridlunds, and for all of us

Once, the steady burning of a sturdy star,
golden, prime, bright.
Then darkness and the enormous wheel
of absence, the reeling weight of it
too much to hold. Then numbness,
the necessary blur of motion,
anything to fill his place: impossible.

At Christmas the tree went up. Maybe
the Vikings lost; it didn't matter.
By spring the world bloomed relentlessly
as usual, surge of blossom, heady earth.
We kept remembering, kept walking,
one foot shepherding the next stumble.

A shift, come summer, all our longing
pulled to something tangible
that said his name: *Jeff*. And it became
the father, *raise high the roofbeams*,
carpenter, as he constructed a gazebo.
And it became the mother, cutting pavers
for the garden on a brick-saw with a diamond tip,
measuring, shoveling Class 5 pebbles, sand and dirt;
and loosening, letting go, as spirit
grew around her.

And it became sister, brother,
wielding hammers
and remembering Jeffrey as they laughed
and bossed the crew.

And it became the aunts
who'd watched Jeffrey grow
and mourned him as their own, adding
their sweat to the earth and stone –
and the uncles both here and elsewhere,
each, too, a part of this.

And it became a slight dark-haired girl
who held herself sometimes
because she'd watched her first love
die, but circling now, intent, around pink star-gazer lilies
with her watering can, an orange monarch
butterfly behind her.

And it became the gardener-healer
and her husband, who planned an arc
of luminous foliage framing that gazebo, so lovely
in their dirt-stained clothes they shone
as deeply as those shrubs and flowers.

And it became a stranger
who became their friend, the shy brick-layer
who never knew their son.

And it became Jeffrey, intelligent,
silent, lion-hearted, present everywhere around us,
examining the yellow light of the azalea,
the deep green yew and purple salvias,
dappled strands of the willow's spreading arms.

And it became all of us, a community of love
large enough to exile loss a few mountains west
for a few minutes or a few months;
small enough to hear Jeffrey's voice there
with us, roots in his family, laughing
as he walked with his God.

Eastern Standard Time 9-11-01

for my NY Irish-born grandparents

In Dublin it is nearly four o'clock
and O'Connell Street is thick
with traffic. School–children throng
the buses home and shoppers exit
Cleary's, pleased with bargains.

Turn the clock back to Eastern time,
New York, 10:00 a.m. The sky rains
high–heeled shoes and light
flaming bodies; ash, chalk, dust,
bone, the grit of ruined things.

Sirens wail from Maine to Iowa
and on CNN, the twin towers explode
again and yet again. Grief
goes off like landmines, unexpectedly,
the woman watching TV stunned by pain.

My Irish cousins gather by the phone
in Donnybrook and Harold's Cross
as evening spreads slow from Dublin mountains,
a dropping of purple, the murmur of rhymes
recited at bedtime, September's long song.

Across the sea, the waiting dead assemble
patiently, knowing they cannot rest
until they're found. Days slide
to weeks; their bodies sway with fatigue.
Margaret, kiss the boys for me.

Numbness. A metallic taste.
The world tilted sideways. The papers
fatten with obituaries,
"Loved to Cook," "Family Man,"
"Sorely Missed by Wife and Son."

Remembering Karen Ann Quinlan

At twenty-one, the clocks stopped.
You hardly aged a day after that.

For ten years, your face escaped
the maelstrom of emotion and event
which pitched its common sediment
and markings on the rest of us.

Now, even at death, no storm exists
that can disturb the calmness
of your placid gaze, or the frame
your young girl's hair makes, falling

like a curtain on the brink
of closing shut the face
that coma had already sealed
ten years back.

What's Said

Everything I just told you was a lie.
The small domesticities of tenderness
in the kitchen, the village where my grandmother
was born, how I only drink socially,
even the angle of light on my child's face
in sleep, a lie.

Nothing ever is as it appears: remember that
as you invent the shade of paint needed
to construct beautiful artifice, or fall
so deeply for the characters in your novel
you disconnect the phone to hold
the long conversation in the living room.

Your teenage daughter smoothes the dent
of her boyfriend's frame from the bed
before you wake, saying nothing;
the body count in the war contains
fabrications; rain's predicted
but it snows; you say "I'm fine, I'm really *fine*
when you aren't, and somewhere
in between lies a fraction of the truth.

Coasting

You get used to it, this endless driving
nowhere through the desert.
The mind becomes slack as windless sand
and shifts to automatic pilot; the land flat,
familiar. Dusk settles and the air
begins to grey –

Oh, you've been here before, the place
where soul slows its breathing
and each day's gestures spin into the next.
The same laundry stack as yesterday
awaits folding, the same novel beckons,
the same bed sighs as you enter it again.

Whatever was sharp, alive or longing
fades. No praises rise for the latest
golden lustrous moon; only the idle strum
of car wheels coasting through territory
too well-known, the day rinsed of meaning
before the morning's half begun.

Brother of Music

I am in love with the voice
of a man who lives down the street.
Cutting through my lawn at night
he sings an old Righteous Brothers tune
a capella as he wanders home:
"Oh, my love, my darling,
I hunger for your touch…"

And the timbre of his notes
clings to kitchen curtains blowing
in the breeze, sets the bedroom rug fur
on end, lays a restless spell
on my twisted summer sheets.
"But time goes by so slowly,
and time can mean so much –
are you still mine?"

August thunder hums, then hesitates
as his clear voice blends with rain
in the darkness at the end of our block.
"The long lonely years…"
A sweet tenor, deep alto
cradling my ears, steaming my bones
like the comfort of hot towels

in a winter without heat
and I want, I want, I want
to whisper from the window
"don't go—"
God speed your love, wherever,
and goodnight, brother.

Hay

How like a drug
this perfumed air is, the sweet, heavy scent
of hay just mown (*"the first cut
the most fragrant of the season,"*)
Susan told me once.

How I want to breathe it
forever, eat it for breakfast, warm
the chill from my bed with the blanket
of its hot smell, jar it to let loose
in the parking lot of Taco Bell, use it
to honey the exhaust of diesel fumes
from the bus ahead of me,
suck in the dense air of it
until I'm drunk with longing
for another whiff.

How like a lover it becomes
with its canny theft of the senses,
how I crave that abandon and surrender
to the thief. How at this moment
I would lie down and stroke
the tendrils of its fresh silk body,
open my mouth to its narcotic tongue
and let it fill my throat with the deep kiss
of new-mown hay.

Late Evening

An ordinary kitchen
at twenty minutes to midnight.
The clock ticks, June air billows
through the windows, the plants
bloom quietly.
I can hear my neck crack
and a plane like mild thunder
hum onward to New York.
Light from the stove falls
on a page of Jane Kenyon's
last book. Dead before 50,
she'll never know what her poems
mean to me.
A neighbor coughs
and mattress springs shift above
as my children turn in sleep.
Bless this stillness,
my hour of writing…
left fist pressed to mouth, pen
held tight between right fingers,
the air a live current
singing silence through the house.

August Storm

for Pat Tromp

It was late, for her −
11:30, maybe.
Now that Marv was gone,
her house was big.
Lightning at my windows
had kept me from sleep,
and I thought of Pat
thirty miles away from here,
alone. Thunder cracks
made me jump as I got up,
and wind whipped the rain
against glass.

At 79 she had grown
suddenly small, and
because she couldn't find
her car the other night
after the poetry reading,
and because I was worried
about us both, I picked up
the phone and called her.

*Are you watching the storm
dear?* she answered
after two rings.

I can see her as we spoke −
the lance of lightning
fierce as it pierced
falling rain once more—
her small knees tucked
beneath her arms
as she serenely welcomed

thunder, listening
through the long night
for birdsong which comes
faithfully as she knew
it would (though I did not),
each blessed morning.

Considering a Pencil

Consider a pencil, that most utilitarian
of tools. School-days, sharpened number-twos,
their dark lead eager to make marks, every
child's zippered bag cradling a few.
Or the carpenter's version, angled and squat,
its blunt point designed for straight lines
crucially drawn and positioned for the saw.
The one-inch stubs an eight year-old brings home,
my artist friend's charcoal-looking one
she uses as she sketches still-life nudes,
the cheap yellow drugstore piece I jot
the boys' heights with on the kitchen wall.
Graphite descendent of the sharpened stone
which carved a people's history on cave walls,
rough cousin to the implement which first touched
the Sistine Chapel's virgin white throat,
or mundane tube of lead an adolescent
moves around the paper's edge
to write "Sue loves Bill, 1999."

Lament

It's clear I've missed a few stellar odes
on my way to do the laundry – cracks
in the canon, Li Po and Heaney's gold.

I make school lunches dressed in black,
heave mustard, ham and mayo on the bread
while pondering what Yeats meant:

What need have you to care (he said) *for wind
or water's roar?* It's evident
he wrote this for a child or adolescent,

the one whose algebra is calling from
another room, who studies hardest after 10:00 p.m.
And now the sink is plugged again... I'm numb.

Done with Auden, ditto Pound. What use is rhyme
or meter when the day is left to climb?

The Men in the Basement

The men in the basement are tired,
they say, of working without a contract.
I've heard their low grumbles in the evenings
as I read by the stove, and the word *union*
has slipped through the floorboards once or twice.

It was easier when there was just one –
mild, handsome Jake who fixed the faucets
when they leaked, bled the radiator pipes in Fall,
hung paintings on the bedrooms walls
and was happy with a plain pork chop dinner,
desserts a few nights a week.

Then Ted knocked one night, his bag of metaphors
slung on one shoulder, the whole bright alphabet
spilling on the threshold. Because the house repairs
were caught up and because the poem
I was working on was a little bare, I let him in.
We talked till dawn in the kitchen, and I swore
I'd only borrow what I needed from his bag,
then made another bed up in the basement.

These days it seems a little servicing
will only go so far. The philosopher complains
I no longer help him wring meaning
from the stars, the accountant disapproves
of the red ink in my books, and my handyman
threatened to move on today when he found
the poet in my bed tucking images inside my pillow.

The trouble with fantasies is that
they become unwieldy, swelling into great,
lumbering bears with large paws
who outgrow their downstairs beds
and begin to roar for more food, more
attention, more me. I hate to add
a locksmith to the mix, but
I need one for that basement door.

Sand Sculpting

What I had built would shift and fall
with the first wind, the first drop of rain.

But still – the feather tied to twig to serve as flag
was satisfying, and with the cup someone had left
I sculpted crimped turrets along the castle parapet.
Despite the sand it seemed a thing as solid
as the swimmers in this cold bowl of mountain lake
or the white geese honking on the shore.

I'd been watching a couple on the beach,
some easy grace of history between them
like a third person, the ordinary freckles
on her cheeks wrinkling into smile
as he turned to her from time to time,
just talking, that was all.
It wasn't that the earth shifted where they sat
or that the obvious perfume of passion hung
around them, but having *known* once the blue calm
of love's house, I recognized it and was hungry
for its entrance, longing for its quiet rooms.

I couldn't, after all, ask whether they'd mind
if I came closer and just stared for a while,
so I continued building my little sand frame,
adding elaborate halls and chiseling a pattern
made by stick on the outer walls, placing goose feathers
above the moat to make the necessary bridge.

Red chips made of plastic cups became the rose garden
because, rubbing sleep from our eyes at sunrise
in the chill of the castle tower
when looking down, a little beauty would be needed.
There was a moment I was pleased with it.

Then I looked up again to two people
on the beach, still in love, still talking.
How I wanted to memorize them!
To have their sheen be mine.

A wave came and added water to the moat,
licking the castle's edge as I started again.

SKY OF THE OTHERWORLD

Tuesday at the Outreach Office

"Te amo hijo mío" Victor tells the child,
a two year-old whose mother has run off.
They're here for help, for county benefits
they can't get without the child's birth certificate.
"No hablo español," I inform the dad
apologetically. Beyond a few stock phrases,
it's the truth. Victor has no English,
I have no Spanish, but the boy
now has a cup of applesauce
and so the dance begins – phone call
after phone call for referrals
to a Spanish-speaking social worker,
and it's 4:00 p.m. I switch on
the speaker phone – finally, a lead,
and a volley of Spanish rains
into the conference room, her voice,
his voice, faster and faster. Victor slows,
hands the phone to me. The little boy
wants his mamá, and we're missing one.
"It's complicated," the social worker says,
"the mother took the birth cert when she left,
the father lost his job because he had no one
to care for his son, they're behind $900 on the rent,
the eviction process has already begun,
the car's hanging on by a tire and a prayer,
and we can't even give him food stamps
without documentation. I'm referring him
to Legal Aid on Thursday." *"Sí,"* I say,
"yes, *yo comprendo.*"
Victor lays his head down on the table
and weeps, a language that we both understand.

Signs

"Homeless, please help, God Bless."

"Will barter for cash."

"Vet on the edge."

"My kids are hungry – did yours eat today?"

"Not gonna lie, I need a quart of beer."

"Please, just bus fare, my feet are killing me."

"Need \$\$ for co-pay on my insulin."

"Keep your coins, we want change."

Loss: An Inventory in Chorus

I lost my shoes and shirt last night,
sleeping at that big downtown shelter
where bodies sprawl mat-to-mat
in the hundreds. I'd used the shirt & shoes
as my pillow; when I woke,
my head was on the floor.

> I'd been doubled up at Jenna's's for a month, sleeping
> on the couch. When the fire came there wasn't time
> to find Anna's baby photos or the one copy of my
> resume on disk. *Start again, my friend*; that old refrain
> I'd come to hate.

I've never lost my vodka bottle
but cell phones? I've lost my share.
The current one is missing
with links to anyone who mattered
and now I think I'll lose my mind.

> What I can carry is a bedroll
> and a few plastic bags.
> The apartment is a memory, those dishes
> with a swirl of cherries on the edge,
> the green velvet couch, my ID
> and birth certificate filed who-knows-where.

I've lost my case manager, she either quit
or traded me for someone else.

> I've lost two toes to frostbite,
> my front teeth to a fight, my girlfriend
> to alcohol, my dog tags to a hole
> in the frayed pocket of a jacket.

Some nights I feel I've lost the dead,
my mother who would come to me in dreams,
her long black hair braided with softest feathers,
the small sun-catcher spilling light
at her throat. Gone now, the dreams;
bow to the streets, our future king.

Eamonn's Story

Addiction the slaver,
obedience, its leash.
Addiction the master, whip raised,
welts after. Addiction the famished,
please feed me, I'm ravenous.
Addiction the lover,
heart scoured clean, *let me in*
let me in, I will carry you, hold you,
act as reprieve until sleep.
Addiction the butcher, knife
severing air until death occurs –
two ragged breaths, then none.
Addiction the hum of stars
gorgeous in their too-bright sockets,
all the constellations loved –
Orion, Charon, the Plieades –
stolen, rearranged by noon.
Addiction, the fair-haired child,
ruined.

Shelter

Lottery

No one talks much during lottery,
all eyes on the Bingo balls
placed in the bowl. I write the numbers
by each man's name on the list.
The names of the men stand for beds,
or the desire for one. Who will win?
There are five spaces here
and three referral slots at Our Savior's.
But there are forty-seven men, and this means
some will get the tramp camp downtown
and sleep badly as they guard their shoes,
some will lay their bodies down outside
under the freeway bridge nearby, and some
will drink Nyquil in the alley until dawn.

Invisible, Among the Men

When Ramon clips his toenails
at the chair beside our table and Tim
scratches his huge belly
above the too-small, on-loan sweatpants
he wears while his clothes spin
in the dryer, I know I am invisible,
a volunteer, another night attendant.
These men are going about their business,
showering and rubbing powder
into athlete's foot, pulling off
their jeans to lounge in boxers,
rearranging their bundled bags
carefully. I look at the floor,
pretend I'm the Thursday nurse
in a boarding school in England,
my long dress and starched cap
blending with the walls.

Cigarette Break

I could smoke all night with them,
Manuel of the clean pressed pants
who thinks I'm from the INS, Manuel
of the earned paranoia; and Billy,
who tells me of the house he owned
two mortgages ago, the repossessed truck
he believes a bankruptcy lawyer
could help him get back. I hand Mike one,
then Lamont, and they're amazed I smoke
at all, much less two brands. I tell them
my story about hedging bets with death,
how when I turned 30 I bought Camel Lights
and tried to alternate with Marlboros,
how I really didn't use the word *death*
to myself but *mortality* instead
because it felt a little vaguer. I light one
more because we all have time on our hands,
because my ten year-old is at his dad's
tonight where he is building a house
under the blanket for his cat, tucking her in
snug; where he will fall asleep holding
what he loves, knowing, even deep in childhood,
there is no greater shelter.

Remembering Luxembourg

The other volunteers don't sleep
well here either. Tonight
I lie awake remembering Luxembourg,
the train station where travellers
could pay to bathe after nights of sleeping rough,
how I put my coins in the slot and felt
such gratitude for water and for soap
that I walked two miles to that small cathedral
on the postcard to think about it all.
Light slanted through stained-glass,

turning the hair on my arms gold.
I remember this: thumb out in the rain
hours later, heading to Switzerland,
I was still warm.

Order

I love the supplies closet, tidiest
of anything here with its rows
of fragrant soap in boxes, bowls
of bright packaged condoms
laid out like mints after dinner,
little sample-size shampoos
and rolls and rolls of toilet paper.
The way the tubes of toothpaste
line up back to back and the razors lie
sharp-side down in their plastic clips
soothes me after what happened
earlier, Kevin screaming
as the paramedics held him down
on the stretcher while they filled a vein
in his arm with Valium
before driving him away.

Refuge

What I know about shelter
is this: nights I've wanted
to phone a friend to ask
for safety, quick, quick, asylum
please, before I lost it all. Some days
I've even had to hide the bullets in the freezer
from myself. Don't tell me shelter
doesn't have arms, substance,
residue. I've been without.
And tasted it.

4:00 a.m.

When there is no light but the gold grid
of stars from the storage closet
patterned on the stained floor,
and no sound but an industrial hum
from the smoke-fan in the hallway
and the quiet turnings of sleeping men
dreaming, perhaps, of their mothers
before turning off the light, or else dreaming
of a different woman reaching for them
once, with love, then it is time for me to wake Miguel
for the long bus ride to his morning shift
in the suburbs, to lay out the Cheerios
and milk on the table and wheel the great vat
of coffee from the kitchen to the hall.

What the Mothers Might Think

Katie of the long red dreads, broken
glasses perched above, if your mother saw the cave
where you live by the river
she would feel the hot knife twist
in her stomach once again. I hear her
stammer *Kate, your mummy bag isn't warm*
enough, your medicine has spilled
into the snow, who will wear
your ballet shoes now?

Jim, you've always said your mother
was a stranger, her eyes lit with meth
and focused squarely down the bright tunnel
of need, unaware your brothers
hadn't eaten yet today. But sometimes
at night in the cold garage where you live,
she shadow-picks at the quilts
that keep you warm, raising her thin wrists
to pull the covers over you; I swear
I've seen her.

Lucky Nan, your mom crooned
when you were just minutes old,
that high, strong cry
pulsing through the caul, the caul
a sign of luck she'd later sew
into your baby clothes, never knowing
you'd be living in a shelter
that doesn't shelter you,
never rocks or sings to you,
forty years down the line.

All the luminous detritus of the past:
red wagon, gleaming; pair of roller-blades
by the door; the prom picture with its shy smile
at sixteen; lock of hair in the envelope;
bronze baseball trophy; Pixie the bear.
Today, a two-inch mat on the floor
as shelter bed; the partly boarded entryway
to an abandoned building where you'll sleep;
perhaps that leafy bit of woods
behind the Goodrich Tires spot. *Mother*, you'll say,
Mary, my mother, this isn't my life at all.

Nicollet Mall Lament

Go to the limits of your longing...
Nearby is the country they call life.

> – Rilke

Her sign say "Homeless," it asks for
"whatever you can give."
She sits on the concrete sidewalk
on Nicollet and 9th without much fuss

though her too-large coat and too-short leggings
make us passers-by wince a bit, avert our faces,
focus on the suit ahead of us or else adjust
our sunglasses. Jessie isn't proud,

she can't ask aloud for cash
or she'd be ticketed as beggar, that archaic term
from Dickens' era. We toss her quarters,
drop a dollar, never ask her what it's like

to live on $203 a month cash assistance
for the indigent plus a spoonful
of food stamps; we don't consider how anyone
can be housed on that amount of money,

instead we wonder secretly why she's out here
on the sidewalk scaring customers away
from businesses again.
It's been a decent day for Jessie,

she's earned $7.00 over four hours
for a Pepsi and a pack of smokes.
Jessie gathers up her things, folds
her cardboard sign and heads back

to the shelter. In the country they call life,
Rilke's ghost slips unnoticed
through the crowd.

Chauncy

Chauncy knew about the plots to kill him, the men on the
bus a jagged flash of light in his side vision; that tightness in
his head as things began to crack and jangle; the loud blue
roar growing in his ears. Sometimes the men followed him
out of the bus back toward the shelter and Chauncy yelled at
them as he tried to knock what they said back to dust. But
that got him kicked out of the shelter, that and a knife he
held up to the pixilated silvery things he imagined that the
men had become. And so he's slept the last two weeks on the
bus bench outside Central Lutheran, and what he's heard and
seen has devilled him each night.

November:

Risperdal quells the rages, Zyprexa the voices and paranoia.
Morning hasn't broken golden yet, and it's still hard for
Chauncy to look you in the eye; almost a kind of shyness.
But no one is following him these days, and his anger rides
lower on his hips. Chauncy is back in shelter, due for
subsidized housing next month, one of the lucky ones. In
his backpack he carries a catalog from a local community
college and for him that catalog is the currency of rubies.
The minutes tick down, and he is counting.

Under the Dunwoody Bridge

On the freeway ramp above, drivers cruise
to 60 mph. Below,
I shove my body past the cop
through a chink in the chain-link fence
that rims the underbelly
of the ramp and I run,
heart thudding, boots hitting chunks of concrete,
heading toward the open-air bed where Maria is.
Her dark hair spills out from under
blankets, and there is her face,
when I lift the covers off, split lips
and puffed-out cheeks, one gash
above her left eye. She is hoarse,
barely coherent as she tries to speak,
her throat dry with fear, *something about Richard.*

Richard is running now, as fast
as the cop who chases him can scream STOP!
Richard dives down to the ground
but keeps one hand in his pocket
looking for god-knows-what
until the cop draws his gun
and kicks him once in the gut.
I shake a little, flashbacks
to a heavy-handed boyfriend of my own.

Two years, Maria and Richard
have lived here two years, and all the small
domesticities are present: pile of books
beside their mattresses, damp pages
furling in the breeze; red suitcase on wheels;
sea of plastic bottles (water, soda, vodka);

a tin dumpster-cubby lined now
with snacks; four pillows, seven blankets,
one monster quilt; someone's frayed stuffed animal;
two green lawn-chairs with torn webbing;
a notebook, three pens, tampons.

❖

Little Tommy Tucker sings for his supper,
What shall we give him? Brown bread and butter.

❖

Light never quite breaches shadow here,
and life beneath the bridge is so far below
the radar of believability
that my body sways a bit, trying to take it in.
20,000 wheels a day steer their way downtown;
in the camps below, the days continue
much like yesterday, invisible, unseen.

❖

Lost in a fog of trauma, Maria won't press
charges later, though as I take her hand now
to stand, she also shakes, remembering
the metal chair he'd hit her with last month,
the rez where she first learned homelessness,
every street that shelter has been absent in
since she turned 14; the nameless men she'd let
prostitute her for a roof those winter nights.
There are only so many broken teeth, so many
memories she can hold. Right now she's cold,
and wants a drink.

❖

The Sandman's coming in his train of cars,
With moonbeam windows and with wheels of stars.
So hush you little ones and have no fear,
Put on your 'jamas and say your prayers.

In the end? There is no end.
There's another bridge at Hennepin,
one at Penn and 394, a half-dozen more
by the river or the light-rail. In this city
and the next, an underworld moves wearily
about its business while AM radio
claims poverty's a myth.
But we are blind to all of them,
the tribe we will not see; we let them be,
we let them.

Dear God of H_____

Oh God of the trumpet red sunrise
burning through the tarp above my tent;
dear God of the warming jeans on the clothesline
hooked between two trees,
God of Dan's sleeping form, let him wake
and light the fire for coffee, let him not
be too hungover from dreams of Gulf War fires
or from Vodka; let peace roll over our small camp
as it deserves to roll.

Lord of Shelterdom, I've been to your floor mats
on Currie Avenue, I've watched
more crack pipes brighten up the street
than the bored security officers have seen;
I've had my shoes stripped from me in the night
and have been punched when brushing past another man's mat
while getting up to use the john. Lord, I've entered
your chapel of the Salvation Army and felt no salvation there
where I've almost spit, God, on *you*, my God on you.

Yaweh of joblessness, when the plant closed
the kids and I became a rudderless boat
careening through deepening waves.
Jonah hates the "shelterbus" ride to school; Jane's too young
to know. Today I walked to Welfare to complete more forms,
then to a market two miles away for dinner things, then
to the diabetes clinic for my check-up. My feet burn,
my toes are fat cows. Holiness, I have no busfare.

Rain down, oh rain down, you desolate
blessed God of homelessness.
You with your large hands,
play it out: bestow on us every clement bit of justice
that you own, for today is a day tender as April,
and it carries the shudder of goodness.

Heat

It is the hour of heat.
I feel it like a pair of giant hands
pressing down the sky. I hear it
like the roar of freeway in my brain.

Somewhere a cat mutters hoarsely from a dream.
Every particle of air gasps for rain.
It is the hour of restlessness,
of prayer, of sweaty tossing

over past lies, promises undone.
All over the city, lightning
dangles like white filament, striking,
missing pavement, car and man.

It is the moment
when a man's hand on Franklin Avenue
might limpen suddenly, a sheen of current
from the knife traveling through his arm.

It is the hour just before the storm
when rain will pound away incestuous tracks
on beach sand, and tomorrow will begin
clean as helium, green as the Atlantic's edge.

The New Place

I slept in a wooded camp three months back,
near a tinny creek behind the impound lot.
Bean cans, bottles, old potato chip sacks
littered the path to my tent, the garbage of others before me.

Someone had dumped a grey van seat,
and rusted springs ripped through
its left side. I used the right side to read
at night, and to whittle during daylight.

Here at the new place it's raining,
but the mottled sky outside and the empty rooms
I stand in are in are beautiful alike, because
I've just signed the lease for my first apartment.

Tomorrow the thrift-store furniture will arrive
at the apartment as planned – couch, lamps,
table and chairs, the double bed with heavy wooden frame,
even two paintings for the kitchen.

At this moment, the wood floors shine
and the tune I hear is a lyric string of notes,
no minor keys. I take in the four walls around me
as light pours through windows, open my throat

and let these words spill out: *warm safe mine.*

Home, Abode, Address

In the dream, winter sun warms the bricks
of rowhouses near the river to a pink glow.
Toilets work. The electricity stays on.
And the table after dinner is a place
for homework before bed.

If I told you what it meant
to have a home, what would you
believe? All the dictionary definitions:
house, abode, address, place to live,
considered one of life's necessities,

structure providing protection
against weather or danger.
These are the basics of housing –
each beloved head upon a pillow,
safe, secure, its rightful place –

dreaming, all of us.

SKY WITHOUT END

Where Acorns Fall

Bury me where acorns fall
from great trees that sway
their hips when winds come
and in the deep heat of June
offer shade for lichened letters
growing from the stone above
my grave, where in December
hard starlight forces shadows
from burr oaks onto snow
and where I will recall the joy
of climbing, my foothold
on the ragged bark a kind
of tense kiss, my body
wrapped around the dark
trunk, nails dug in tight
for life.

Fireflies

Surge and dim, the fireflies
say, here is our light,
our brief hum; look twice,
we're gone.

I remember the sky thick
with them in childhood,
their soft throb of yellow
glowing above the barn
where the woods begin.
My father helps me
catch them, one small spark
at a time. We cup a lid
on their fire in the jar,
then I take the wealth
inside, but the airholes
aren't big enough
and in the morning
they're dead bugs
again. My dad nods,
he's seen it before.

What made me think
I could keep fire?
What made me think
I could keep anything,
much less desire?

Now my father's head
is being mapped for radiation,
lines drawn across his throat,
a helmet fitted to his skull
to chart the space of flesh
the doctors want to burn.

Little errant cells have hid
before the surgeon's scalpel
and have migrated now
to a distant lymph node
to begin another life.

The light of a man
dimming. The tall pine
my father was, the fire in him
bright as fireflies blinking and hiding
and blinking their brilliance again
inside green-needled limbs.
Now his grey branches
stoop with snow, all the sparks
asleep, breezing away
so gently by degrees through the night,
fire blown to the winds.

The Scholar in the Playroom

My father's head was propped up in his hands.
Around him chaos swirled; the cello played
off-key in practice, someone vacuumed sand
we'd tracked in from the beach. I was amazed

that he could concentrate through all of this,
scoring Shakespeare's words with yellow pen
and calmly reading as I wrestled Fergus
while the youngest blundered through the den.

For years I've carried my father's image around,
the flame in the storm who loved the crazy wind
his children were despite the din of sound
he sometimes wished he could rescind.

He proved the ivory tower a myth, this anti-Lear,
who kept his children, his Cordelias near.

Nothing Gold

Everything my father's loved is leaving –
the taste of whipped cream dessert
at lunch; the bloom of Russian sage
in the August garden; the words
to his beloved Emily's poems;
that Irish tune my mother used to hum.

Tonight he thinks he is a prisoner, poisoned
by my older sisters, whose names he can't recall.
On the telephone he sounds afraid and frail.
Voice low, he asks when I can come to get him, do I know
the street number of the house where he is being held,
how soon, God help us, can I get there?

And I am desperate not to hear this story, wild
to seize him from the place where his brain flares
and slows, just as his gait, too, has slowed
to shaky, baby steps that inch their way
out to the car in the driveway.

Mind back, he whispers to me
"Nothing gold can stay," and I recall him
quoting Frost or Yeats at the dinner table
for his nine children through the years,
recall how poems lived in the house
in all the rooms my father walked.
So dawn goes down to day...

And oh my father, at this moment
I would welcome the wolves
from that fairy tale you used to tell,
would gladly let the day end with you
tucked upon their sled
headed toward the dark woods –
oh, I'd believe all their promises to take care
of you, I'd believe anything they said.

Ladybug, Ladybug

Just a speckled heartbeat of a bug,
but what a hardy one he is, his domed body
suctioned to the side window of the car
as I drive for forty miles now
on this county road, bemused by my companion.

He must be frightened by the gusty truck-wind
as the semis slide by us, must tremble
as the air current rocks his small body
like the waves of the ferris wheel on Navy Pier;
his shell must be chilled even in the strong April sun.

I watch his legs, small as eyelashes, move
an inch every now and then, picking their way
down the cliff-front of the car until they rest
on the lip of rubber that abuts the glass, where
he tests my attention by playing dead.

What spunk this little bug owns,
the strength of lions scaled down
to the diminutive, every cell of him
intent on holding on.

Passage

for C., in his kindergarten summer

His first baby tooth out, no bigger
than a quarter of my pinky nail –
with a pin-prick hole, browning now,
where once it sucked upon a root.

I touch the empty socket in his mouth
and marvel at the soft gap there,
the tiny V-depression in his gum.
Earlier, he'd plied me with his wonderings:
"what does the fairy do with all those teeth,
Mom? If she planted them, would they grow

again? Maybe if she washed them first
she could give them to the new babies
without teeth…" At 10:00 p.m.
he's finally sleeping, dreaming
of that tooth fairy, her gauzy wings
and fat, clinking purse.

I place this nugget of his childhood,
a midget-sized, already greying artifact,
on the white tundra of counter-top
and press its dead baby sharpness
against my skin.

Late now, the hour begs for transformation
from this lump of mortal, tired flesh I am
into the realm of parent magic.
Strapping on the heavy wings of myth
across my shoulders, I stoop to straighten
wrinkles from my frayed costume.

How can I ever let him age beyond
five years? Behind me drags the weight
of an ancient purse; before me,
the long three yards from the doorway
to his pillow. Conor,
I grow older.

Because of Them

Before words had formed
beneath the pulsing fontanels
on their infant skulls,
during the years they slept
through damp-haired Julys
and two-blanket Decembers,
through nights & nights of *please Mom,*
one more story and later, the yawning length
of *Tom Sawyer* and *Harry Potter* aloud;
before the blonde girls with restless eyes
began to call, while my sons' bodies
lengthened in their beds as they slept
and their faces changed from boys
at night to men at dawn –
men who spoke the sudden secret tongue
of new initiates, laconic monosyllables
and the speech of turned shoulders –
all this time I went about my life
and cast my nets into the future;
my mother-threads invisible
but sewn lightly to their shoulders
for a time when they might turn
to tug those threads and I would heed the pull,
I would reach backward to the moment
before I even knew their names, I would leave
everything and come to them.

Waiting Up

They're late, a full hour later
than they said they'd be, and they're at it
again – the run-and-ditch fireworks
set off with friends in the park, which summon
the cop car's blazing lights and draw the midnight ire
of neighbors. Or else they've missed their ride home
from the movie, and now are kissing girls in a dark alley,
girls who boldly push their large breasts forward
against my boys' skinny teenaged chests.

There's my father thirty years back, waiting his heart out
each weekend night as we turned 15,
turned 16, then 17, a flock of daughters
turning and laughing, coming and going, leaving
and coming back again so many hundreds of times
while he slept at the kitchen table with his head
on the book, one hand reaching outward
in the pose of a man who is tired but wants to be ready –
the lights dim but the father present
there, a force with whom we must reckon.

As I wake on the couch at this late hour
when my sons return, will they know
I've memorized the clock again, have spun the threads
of their imagined disasters to the spool's end,
that I've been waiting up for them again,
my father's daughter yet?

The Laundromat Man

He's a tumble of earth-tones, brown
and green, a shirt flying sideways,
grey-shades, lean. He's a malleable face
and wild silver-brown hair, bending down
like a boy to pull jeans from a dryer.
He's a messenger-bag guy
stuffing socks in his sack,
a torrent of moon-glow
lighting his back.

And me? I am silent, my small bag of want
clean as detergent, gaining weight
by the second without my consent;
disturbed by desire for the laundromat man
and September's first stars as they rise
and blaze by the moon.

Ghazal

Say your kisses are small fires on the hillside
of my throat. All night the flames, the heat, the light.

This morning sun seized the mountain by degrees,
spreading neck to feet its lusty jewelry of light.

Your body underwater in the clear-bottomed lake
stuns me as it loops through scallops of electric light.

The hummingbird just now, stopped in its own air-current.
Before any touch, a blurred vision, a hovering of light.

Trace the imprint of the snail fossilized in stone, the whorls
frozen, and know the heart petrified, deprived of light.

I want to know what print your tongue will make on mine,
what new alphabet desire might create, its weight, its light,

And why speech becomes a useless coin, a kind of poverty
when you enter me, that note of high-pitched singing light.

An unbearable geography, this land of longing; the tension
of a song trapped in stone. Blaze, stone, then liquefy to light.

Even in the uterus before birth I knew—
I saw the verge of egg and sperm exploding into light

And wanted nothing more than this: to follow it, your kiss
    upon my throat.
Dear God, I swear I've spent my *lifetime* being faithful to this light.

My Childhood Husband

My childhood husband, I loved you first at 10
when you picked me for the kickball team
and bucked me on your new red 3-speed
over half the town.

At 13 your height caught up to mine
and your shoulders grew wide. Hair sprouted
from your soft cheeks, and you moved three parishes
away. I buried an empty matchbox in the yard.

Seasons scattered; we turned east, west, put on
our adulthoods separately. I married first, then you,
then you again, then me. Children, stonework, poems,
gardens, cancer, houses, travel, years.

Tonight I look at all 57 years of you,
remembering how we'd memorized
each other's souls those summers in the treehouse.
Come to me, love; every year begins and ends here.

Swannanoa Afternoon

For Eleanor Wilner

Under the vine-cloaked trees
a June wind rains down orphaned leaves,
pin-oak and palm-sized maple,
scraps of locust. Through the slats

of the bench where I sit, ivy sinews
upward, lacing a pattern of new green
against the weathered old. I'm in that idle
weightless state of watching everything

and watching nothing, thinking at once
of my dead parents, of the bee hovering
near my foot, the vagaries of solitude
and the far drone of cars on the mountain road,

of that time I told my youngest child
that love was worth risking everything
and then lived my days in careful distance
from that declaration.

A ladybug alights on my wrist,
deliberate, speckled, beautiful.
It is so peaceful here alone,
the blurred croak and hum of bullfrogs

by the pond, birdsong
layering the air in different keys.
Now the lemon finch I've been tracking
lands nearby, then ascends; shreds

of a nest-in-the-making drifting from its beak.
I reach and finger what the bird has left me,
hold its difficult weight of goldenness, of dun.
Oh irony, the flattened years when

I expected nothing – then this slow tilt
toward meaning in the small.
Move, the bird seems to urge
And I do.

The Lost Sisters

One by one they fall,
some to blunder, some to scorn,
but absent, at the end,
as my best red dress was the year
it disappeared from the closet
when the wild squirrel
left shreds of chewed fabric
strewn across the floor.

I remember the slam-dunk energy
of their childhoods, and the tenderness
with which they fought to please me then.
And here they are now, at my door tonight,
same long braids, same laughter,
same chewing gum. They swirl around my room
at this late, late hour, in their mismatched pajamas,
long-limbed and beautiful, wanting just to stay up
and talk a little while longer. All the innocence of the past
lingers with them here; and it is not yet the future,
when what will happen settles in my throat…

Those girls—how I loved them
when they crooned the Beach Boys' *Sloop John B*
to their make-believe mikes while rocking back
and forth for the crowd. How I loved
them later, when I saw their own infants
being born; learning something with those births
of the altered world.

Why is it that sisters draw blunt lines
in dust and our shoulders turn to stone?
I feel all history flattens then,
all survivors weep into the anger-stained fields.

Whatever I thought I knew – I didn't.
My job is to rescue my sisters as they fall
and breathe life back to their mouths
from the fire that I own. When they mistake me
for the enemy, when their eyes
implore me not to shoot, I'll whisper *no, my girls,*
oh, no; I'd never harm you.

Perhaps I do love them still,
those lost sisters –our distances benign;
only the same wound speaking
as my own; only the same harsh voice
not telling me they care.

Artifacts

Coming across them unexpectedly like that
after years

birch bark tendrils, translucent
as an uncoiled sigh in sleep

a sack of forest twigs breathing
forest tang before air grows factual again

small gift, first offerings
the past bursting into present tense

a shock   sudden as the notes of Beethoven
crashing through the dark hallway

or the single quiet night we swam
surprised as fish inside each other

troubled
as we rubbed uncertain gills

by a presence of death in things unsung
the incense still packaged

notes from an old sonnet
shelved before done.

Banishing Mother Judas

Two, I answered, *I have two*
children. Then the air shifted.
I put my wine glass down.
My throat felt thick, as if
I'd swallowed the third child whole.
A cock crowed twice.

We leave the picnic, two boys
and I, Conor's hand grazing mine,
the pucker of Naoise's lips, whistling.
Somewhere in a room away from here
another mother strokes the freckles
on our child's face; I hear his high voice
reeding out her name, not mine. His absence
swells until it becomes its own ghost
walking the three of us home.

If we could start again, small one,
when you were just born – take back
my arm, its weight of goodbyes –

On the road, a springer slowly limps by us,
maybe weighed down by his load of age,
and I fight the feeling that it's my job
to strap the dog upon my back when he tires,
to know his stagger and torn muscle
as if it were my own. But I'm no Christ,

just an ordinary woman
whose arms slipped from holding too much
human weight. And I'm not Judas, either,
robes heavy with betrayals. I am the mother
of three children, two beside me now, one
a son whose star graces two roofs,
another's and my own.

A stone's throw from the house
rain begins and the boys run for the door.
At my feet the wet rocks glisten red, then brown.
I bend down and scoop a light handful up,
then drop them in my pocket, pebble-
gems I'll polish once home.

In My Father's Voice

"Remember that quote from James? Letters, in the New Testament?
It's a poor paraphrase, but something about the man who owns two coats
being a thief when the second man has none."

"But what's it for, except to give away,
to give it back? There's nine of you, a lot,
and my conscience veers left and right
each night, wondering whether
my small sums should go to you
or charity. When those voices come
I give it up to trust, to what we left
you, what was taught.

How I worry! That your children
won't collect Social Security, that
their children will be bankrupt.
Worry stalked me from the cradle, my father
dead at 35. Eleven, the oldest, I felt
the clocks seize that instant
but the worry kept on ticking.

God, am I wrong to want a new roof
for Áine, a safer car for Kate, college-help
for Seán, some family boost outside the palms
of the IRS *and* a shelter for the homeless
made of bricks and heat and beds,
real dollars, not just sentiment?

Dear Hearts, the same old lessons, I'm afraid,
from the same old man: feed the hungry.
Clothe the shivering. Fix your furnaces,
and pay off the Visa animal breathing
at your necks. But don't forget
the whole wide world alive and wanting,
the humming need of it. I love you,
do you know that? Give it back."

For What We Cannot Name

"Thou Before Whom Words Recoil..."

The old Hindu mystic knew
how spirit waves goodbye
and vanishes when captured,

the way the green luna moth
diminishes inside the case
to bright shell only.

Today as fog loops
around blue mountains
and evaporates,

I am mute again
because the words *praise*
and *awe* remain mere words

when the plain pod
of lupine seeds
I hold in my palm

carries next year's
wild purple
ticking in its husk.

ETHNA MCKIERNAN has been twice awarded a
Minnesota State Arts Board grant in poetry, most
recently in 2011 for the completion of *Sky Thick
With Fireflies.* McKiernan's first book *Caravan*
(Dedalus Press and Midwest Villages & Voices,
Minneapolis) was a Minnesota Book Award
Nominee. Of her second book, *The One Who
Swears You Can't Start Over* (Salmon Poetry), *The
Bloomsbury Review* wrote, "McKiernan seems to
write because she has to, and graces her verse with
resonance because she can. She stands out among
the ranks of poets for her ability to match language
to subject, sound to sense." McKiernan ran an Irish
book distribution business (Irish Books and Media)
for over two decades and has worked the past four
years for a non-profit serving the Minneapolis
homeless. She holds an MFA from Warren Wilson
Program for Writers.